Mickey Baker's COMPLETE COU[RSE]

jazz guitar

A Modern Method in How-To-Play Jazz and Hot Guitar

To Rector Bailey
A Great Friend and Teacher

LESSON 1

Chord Forms

Below we have all the chord forms that will be used during this course of study. However, other chord forms will appear which are already familiar to you.

We are not dealing with rhythm (foundation) chords because rhythm and standard harmonic progressions will come from other sources, such as the piano, bass or another guitar. What we are interested in is the application of the modern harmonic sound offered by the "Upper Partials".

Try fingering these chords and familiarize yourself with them. Their movement will be applied starting in lesson 2.

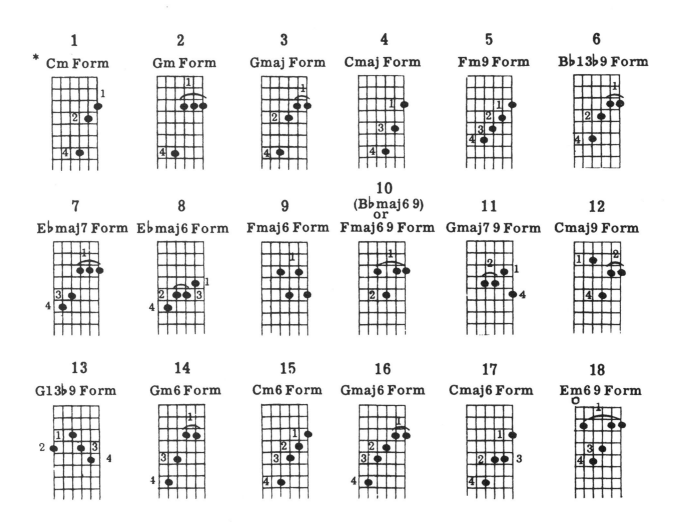

* If these Forms are too hard to finger in this position, move them up to a higher chord such as: Eb ⎰maj or A ⎰maj.
⎱mi   ⎱mi

LESSON 2

Chord Forms cont'd

These structures are called "Chord Forms" because they move from one form to another by sustaining certain tones and moving others freely up or down the finger board, as seen in examples 1 through 4 below.

Your fourth finger plays a major part in forming these structures, therefore, the examples below are to be practiced chromatically from the first to the tenth fret on your guitar.

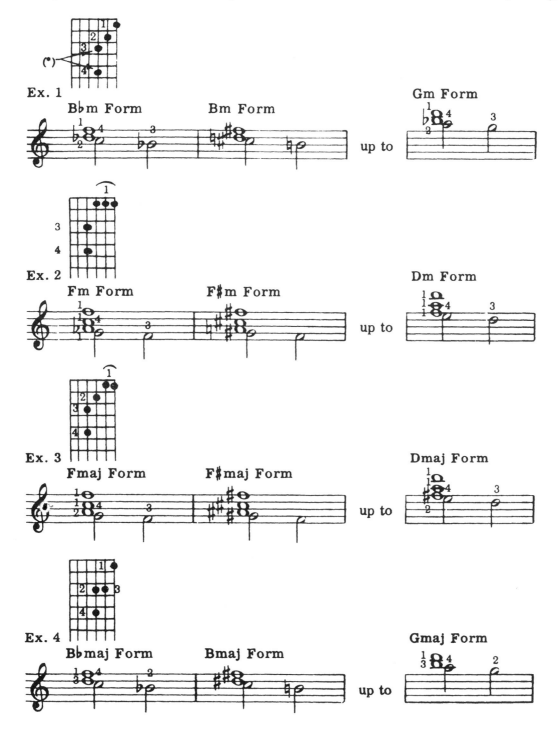

* Notice that the bottom tone of <u>each</u> <u>chord</u> moves down a whole tone.

Chord Exercises

By now your fourth finger should be pretty sore from the exercises in lesson 2. However, once you have gone through this series of exercises you will have closed the gap between Modern and Standard guitar playing.

In this lesson we deal with the same exercises with a moving line below the chord. This exercise in diagram form (example 5) appears strange, but when you realize that the bottom line is moving in single notes, there is no problem.

Practice exercises 1 thru 8.

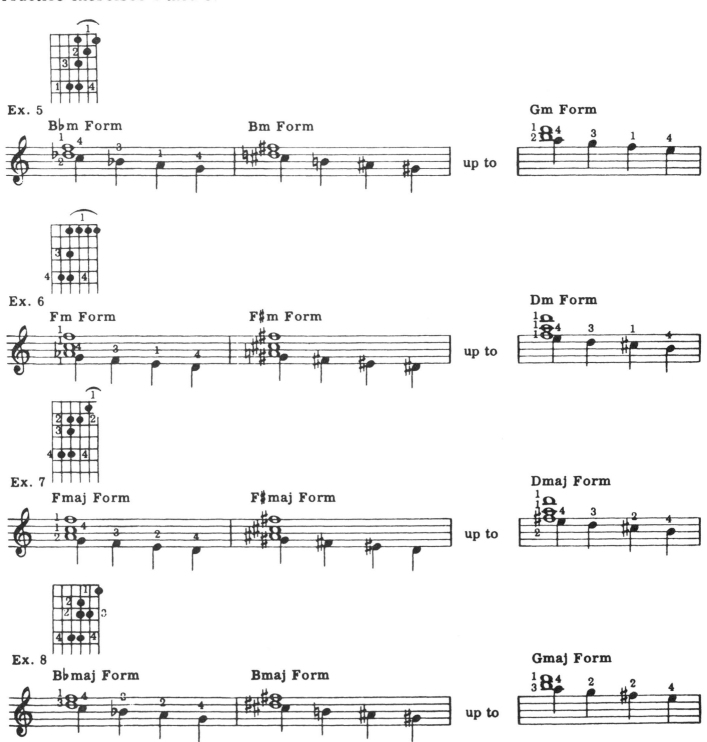

LESSON 4

Simple Chord Analysis

Lessons 2 and 3 involved only eight chords, Nos. 1, 2, 3, 4, 14, 15, 16 and 17.

The exercises start at the first position and you must stretch your fingers a full five frets. I know that this is not an easy project, however, eventually it will become easy for you. In the meantime, if you find it difficult to start in the first position with these exercises, start at a higher position, either the fourth or fifth.

Actually, chord 1, through use of passing tones, resolves into chord 15. Chord 2, through use of passing tones, resolves into chord 14. Each chord is moving from a minor ninth to a minor sixth chord, via passing tones. Chords 3 and 4 are resolving into chords 16 and 17. Each chord is moving from a major ninth via passing tones, to a major sixth. The only difference in these two forms is the mode (major and minor).

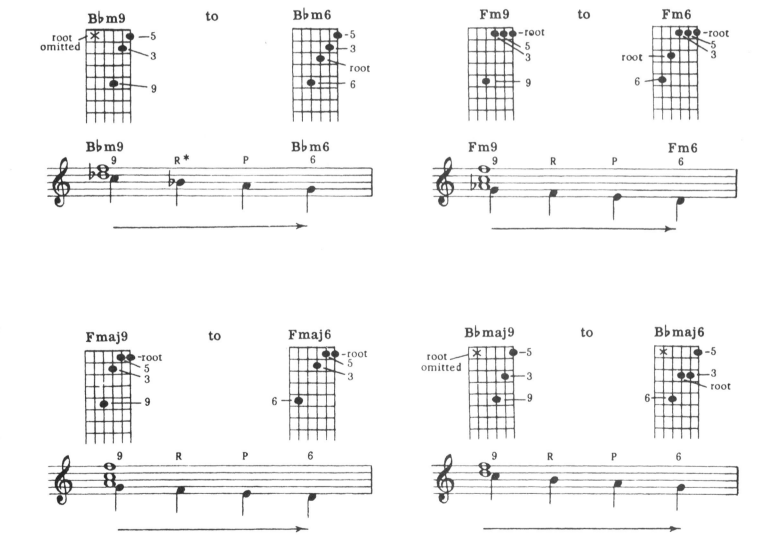

*"R" is for Root, "P" is for Passing tone.

LESSON 5

Chords and Passing Tones

I know that at this stage these chord progressions are still exercises to you, however, I'd like to give you an insight as to their application in modern harmony.

Below you have two exercises putting into play the eight chords you have been practicing. They are written as I always write exercises, with the standard chord progressions on the first line and the modern progressions on the second line.

In exercises 10 and 11 you are moving from a minor ninth to a minor sixth and from a major ninth to a major sixth, although the standard chord structures only move from dominant to tonic.

Analyze the examples thoroughly, practice them chromatically, moving up and down the finger board, moving from minor to major, just as they are written.

Ex. 10

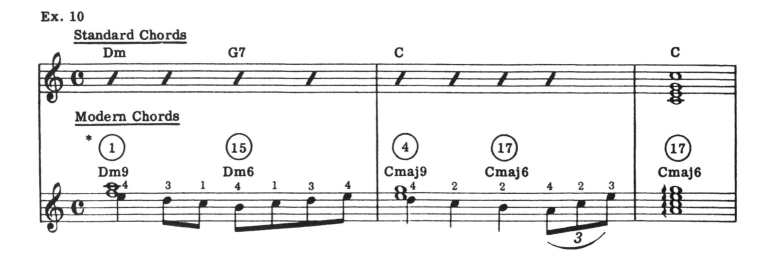

Ex. 11

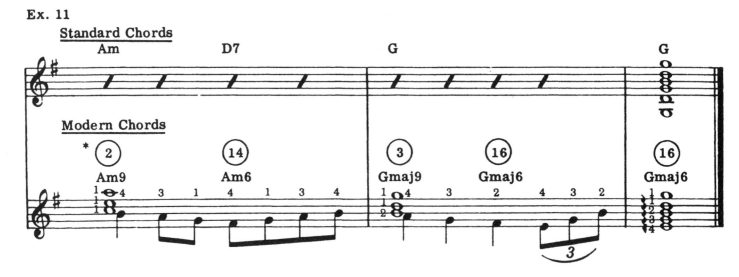

*The circled numbers over each chord indicates which chords are to be used from the chart in Lesson One.

LESSON 6

Dominant to Tonic

CHORD PROGRESSIONS

The chord exercises in lesson 6 will probably be much easier to form and finger than those of the previous lessons. In fact, the most difficult progressions are now behind us. The idea now is to weave these progressions into beautiful music.

We will now take chords 5, 6, 7 and 8 and form a musical cycle which resolves from V, the dominant, to I, the tonic. In this case V to I is from B♭ to E♭. Practice this chromatically up and down the fingerboard.

Exercise 12 below is diagrammed the same as exercises 10 and 11 in lesson 5. The numbers over the chords should tell you at a glance what chords you are to play from the chart in lesson 1. It would do you a lot of good to analyze each of these chords to determine what tone of the chord each note represents and which tones are omitted.

Ex. 12

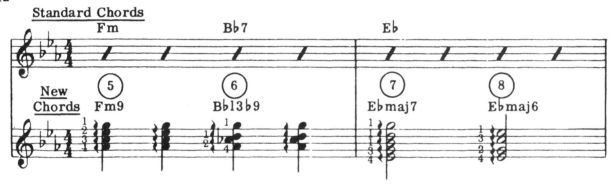

In any of these Exercises (Ex. 10, 11 and 12) the standard chords could have been as follows:

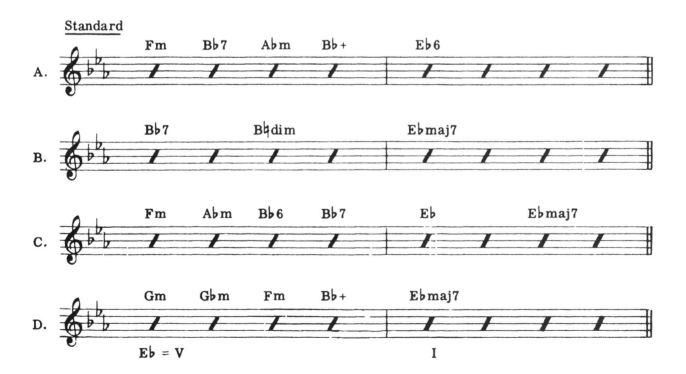

There are many different ways to close a cadence but the "New Chords" in Exercises 10, 11 and 12 will suffice for all. This is only the beginning. There are still more colorful ways of closing a cadence.

Chords and Song Forms

Now that you have a general working knowledge of about half of these chords, let us try applying them to song forms. In this lesson, I have taken a few bars from two well known standard tunes and applied chord 1, 4, 15, and 17 to them.

Exercise 13 is similar to exercises 10 and 11 in lesson 5, the only difference is that in this example we are applying the chords to a song form rather than an Exercise.

In exercise 14, though we are using the same four chords they progress in a slightly different way. In both cases you are starting with the major or minor 9th and closing with the major or minor 6th. These exercises are slowly developing into what is musically termed "Counterpoint", meaning, two lines "Playing" against one another. As we go along we will discuss Counterpoint in more detail.

THIS LOVE OF MINE

Ex. 13

FRANK SINATRA
HENRY SANICOLA
SOL PARKER

© Copyright 1941 Embassy Music Corporation   Used by Permission

I DREAM OF YOU

Ex. 14

MARJORIE GOETSCHIUS
EDNA OSSER

© Copyright 1941 Embassy Music Corporation   Used by Permission

* Each time a chord is diagramed, the first finger falls behind the fret that represents the position the chord is in. In Ex. 13 the first chord is Dm6 9, which is in the fifth position.

Resolution of Chord Cycles

Before we tackle any of the remaining chords, let us get a thorough knowledge of how to apply those we have already worked with. This is not an easy project because it deals with harmony and, as you know, this is not a harmony book. Nevertheless, I will attempt to explain the movement of some of the principal chord cycles in music.

At this point the cycle in which we are most interested is from dominant V to tonic I. Now the question is, what is the V and the I? The V of a chord demands resolution, the I is final. In other words, once you have played the I the ear is satisfied. Any chord that you play during the course of a cycle demands some kind of temporary resolution until it eventually reaches the V (dominant the most active chord of the tonality) and the V resolves into the I (Example 16.)

There are many courses to take through chord cycles that will lead to the dominant and tonic. One of the most popular cycles is from I to IV to V and back to I (Example 17.) Another popular example, and the one in which we are most interested, is from I to II to V to I (Example 18.)

Commit these exercises to memory because in lesson 9 we will approach the art of substituting minor II chords for dominant V chords.

Ex. 16

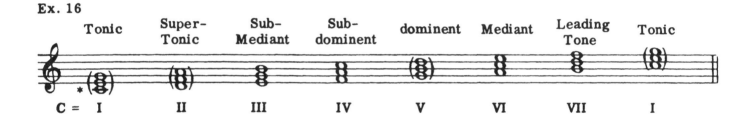

Tonic	Super-Tonic	Sub-Mediant	Sub-dominant	dominent	Mediant	Leading Tone	Tonic
C = I	II	III	IV	V	VI	VII	I

Ex. 17

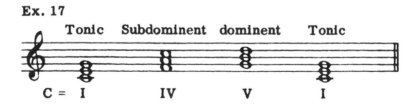

Tonic	Subdominent	dominent	Tonic
C = I	IV	V	I

Ex. 18

| C = I | II | V | I |

* The chords in parenthesis are the ones we are interested in for the present.

LESSON 9

Related Chords

Many chords are closely related to one another. For instance, the C6 chord and the Am7 chord have the same tones. They are called relatives for this reason (Example 19.)

The G9 chord and the Dm chord are relative because the three tones that form the Dm chord are the upper three tones of the G9 chord (Example 20.)

When there is a chord progression that moves only from dominant to tonic, it is possible to use the II chord instead of the V and resolve into the V from the II (Example 21.) For instance, if you are playing in the key of C Major and you have one bar of "C", two bars of "G7", and one bar of "C", (Example 22) it is possible to use the progressions in Example 22 Parts A B C and D. Notice how in each of these examples we add more chords to the cycle yet, basically, the chords move from I to V and from V back to I.

There are many different ways to conceive chord progressions. One thing that you should always bear in mind is, no matter how many chords you add to the cycle, they should eventually reach the dominant and from there resolve into the tonic.

Ex. 19

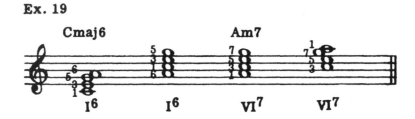

Ex. 20

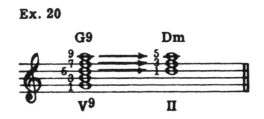

Ex. 21

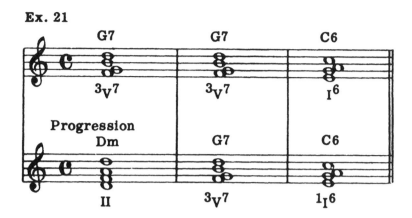

Ex. 22

Ex. 22a

Ex. 22b

Ex. 22c

Ex. 22d

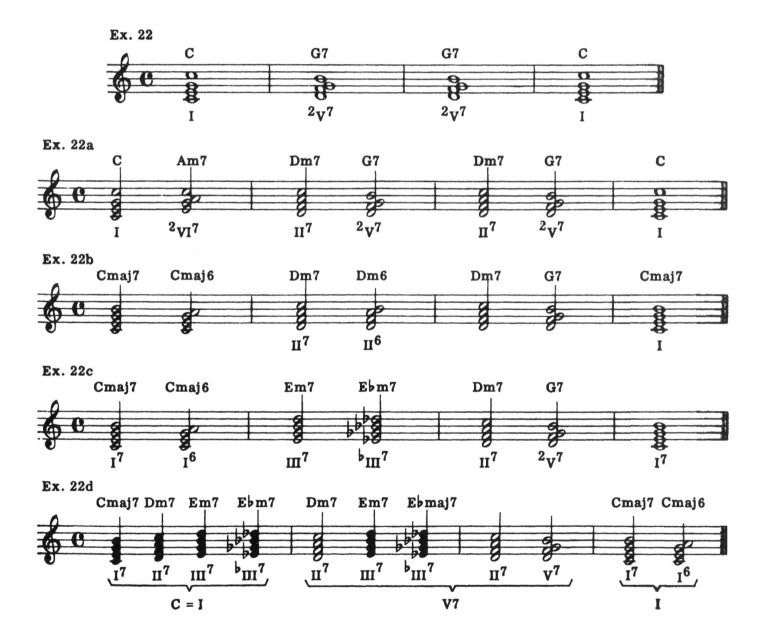

LESSON 10

Altered Chords

Example 22 A B C and D have in them what is known as "Forced Harmony" (adding chords via progressions that move away from, then lead back into the tonic.) It keeps the music active rather than letting it die on a "C" or "G" chord as it was originally written. These are the things that Jazz musicians love to do, and by doing so give a song new color.

Now that you know that the II chord can be readily substituted for the V, let us discuss the "Upper Partials" of these chords. The dominant chord can be the dominant 7th, 9th, 11th, aug. 11th or 13th. The 5th or the 9th can be Flatted, nevertheless, these are still the "Upper Partials" of the dominant chord (Example 23.) They can be used to resolve into the tonic. With the II chord of the scale the same principal applies, you have the 6th, 7th, 9th, 11th, and 13th. Any of these forms of the II chord can be used to resolve into the V which in turn resolves into the tonic (Lesson 7.)

We will not discuss this phase of Chord Cycles any further, however, most of the cycles in this book deal with these principals so I would suggest that you review lessons 8 through 10 frequently.

Ex. 23

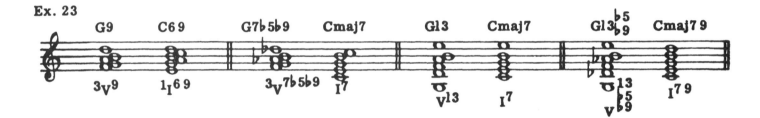

LESSON 11

Chords and Melody Playing

Now that you have a general knowledge of how new cycles can be substituted for the original chord cycles and how the Upper Partials of the dominant can be used to resolve the dominant chord into the tonic, along with the knowledge of II resolving into V, let us get back to chord and melody playing. In the next few examples I will employ as much of this knowledge as possible.

One thing must be made clear to you. When writing an arrangement for a song, which is exactly what you are doing when you make up a chord melody solo, you use the ideas and musical sounds that sound best to you rather than the ideas and chord cycles that were originally written for the song. The original chord progressions of the song are routine and much is left to your imagination. For example, when listening to a Jazz arrangement of a standard song, the chord progressions used in most cases are foreign to the original progressions written for that song, as I pointed out in lesson 10.

In the examples to follow we will employ a variety of chord cycles that can be forced against the original cycles, using fragments of the same songs illustrated in lesson 7, along with a few others. In each example, you have the song fragments as they would appear in sheet music along with two variations.

Master them all, commit them to memory and use only those which you like the best.

THIS LOVE OF MINE

Ex. 24

FRANK SINATRA
HENRY SANICOLA
SOL PARKER

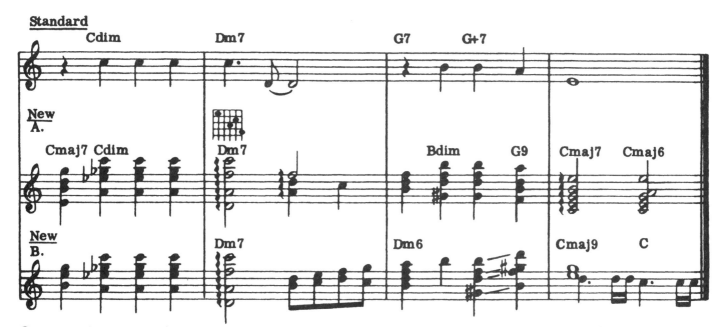

* See Lesson No. 12 Dim. and Aug. Resolutions.

I DREAM OF YOU

Ex. 25

MARJORIE GOETSCHIUS
EDNA OSSER

* See Lesson No. 15.

THERE ARE SUCH THINGS

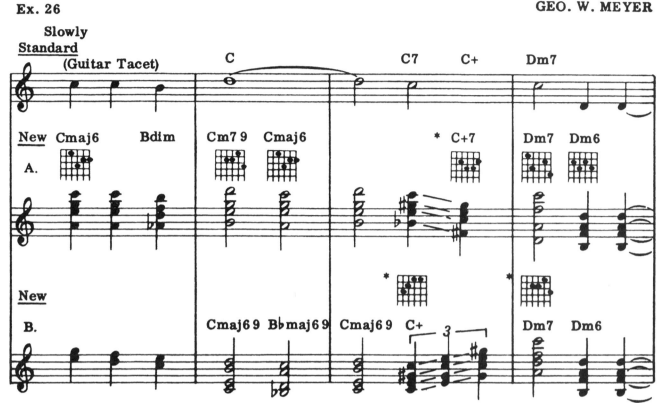

STANLEY ADAMS
ABEL BAER
GEO. W. MEYER

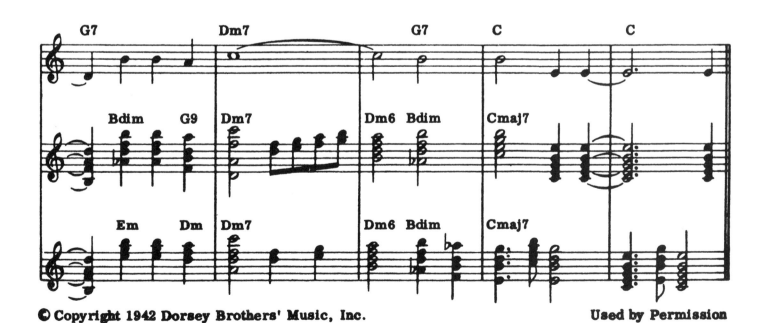

*See Lesson No. 17 "Augmented Cycles".

*See Lesson No. 17 and Lesson No. 23.

EVERYTHING HAPPENS TO ME

MATT DENNIS
TOM ADAIR

Ex. 27

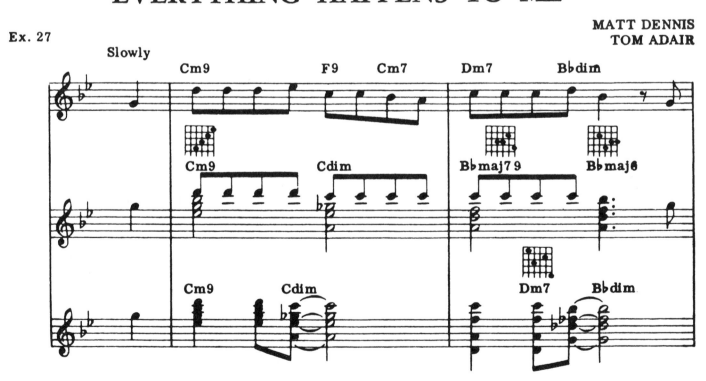

Ex. 28

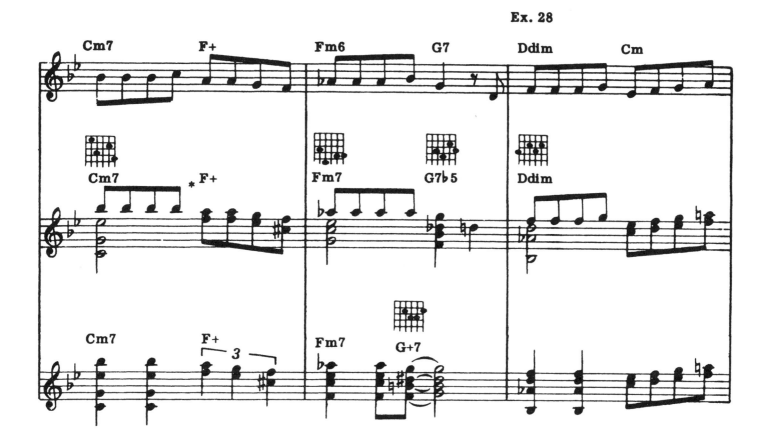

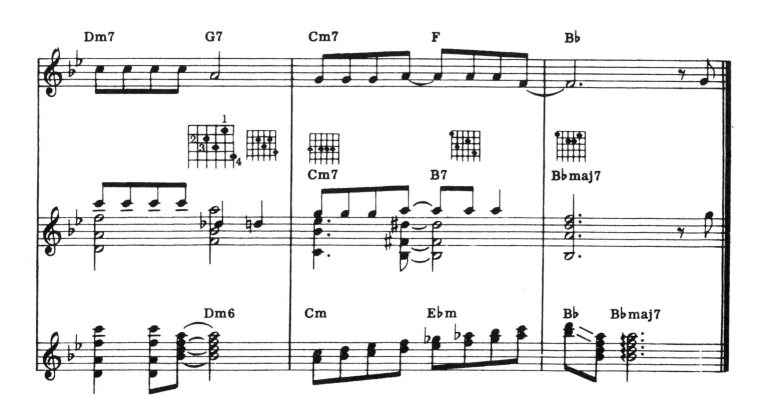

*See Lesson No. 17.

LESSON 12

The Cadence

Most popular music is written in either eight or sixteen bar sequences. At the close of these sequences there is a "Cadence" which ends a musical thought. This is done by progressing into the dominant chord of the tonality and from there into the tonic. We call this the "Authentic Cadence".

The sequence does not have to be eight or sixteen bars. There are introductions and endings in which the "Authentic Cadence" appears that only consist of one or two bars. The difference between an introduction and an ending is that the introduction stops on the V (Example 29). From this point you approach the first chord of the song. An ending approaches the V and moves on to the I, which is the final statement.

Below in exercise 29 there are three examples which are introductions, because the last chord is the dominant or V chord. In exercise 30 these same examples are used but now they are endings because they make a final statement and close with the tonic (I).

INTRODUCTIONS

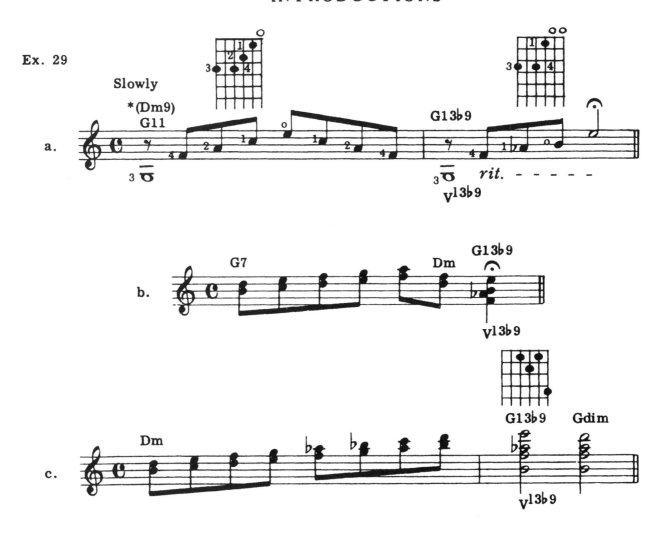

*See Lesson No. 23, Pedal Point.

Ex. 30

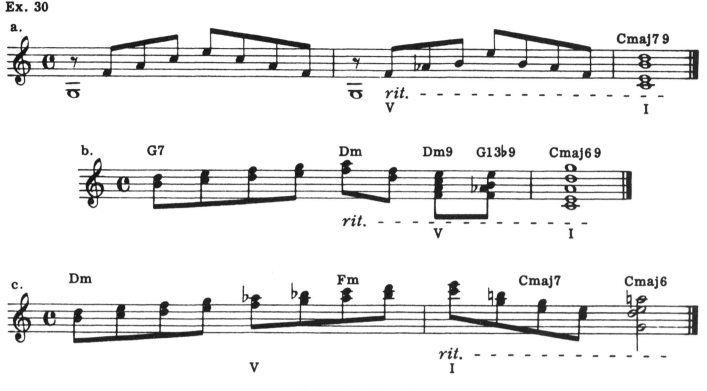

LESSON 13

Symetric Harmony

Symetric Harmony differs greatly from Diatonic Harmony. There is no key signature involved in Symetric Harmony and chords progress freely in this system of music.

We are not interested in the extreme ends of Symetric Harmony, however, there are a few things that can be done on the guitar that create "tremendous" effects. This harmony is introduced into the picture at the "Cadence". With endings you use the Symetric Harmony at the tonic chord. In eight and sixteen bar sequences it is used at the "Cadence" breaks.

In this lesson we have a diminished 7th chord which moves freely up and down the finger board in minor thirds. Exercise 31 illustrates the chord in its proper position all the way up the finger board. Simply follow the diagram and read the musical examples directly below it. See Exercise 31. Notice that below each chord of the musical example there is a small "T" and a number. The "T" represents the word, "Tonic"; the number represents the tonic chord being employed.

As I mentioned before, there is no key in Symetric Harmony, therefore, every chord you play is, in actuality, the tonic. There can be as many tonics as you desire in Symetric Harmony. In order to avoid confusion, in this example and the examples to follow, we will use only 4 tonics; starting with "T1" and ending with "T1" an octave higher. This divides the 12 tone scale into 4 equal parts.

A diminished chord is built on a succession of minor thirds. If you play a diminished chord on the guitar and move it up a minor third, the same tones will appear but in a different arrangement, which means, each tone in the chord is actually the root or the tonic (See Exercise 31b).

Ex. 31

a.

T1   T2   T3   T4   T1

ANALYSIS

b.

Gb Eb A C   A Gb C Eb

LESSON 14

Symetric Cycles

In this lesson we have 4 examples of Symetric Cycles. It isn't necessary to write them in full detail. Only the first chord will be diagrammed and those to follow, as you should know, are a minor third higher.

In exercise 32 the fourth finger moves from the 2nd to the 3rd string as diagrammed. Simply follow the same fingering as you progress up the finger board in minor thirds. These exercises can be extended still higher if you have a Cutaway guitar. If not, carry them as high as your guitar will allow.

Any chord can be played in a Symetric Cycle. Take any of your favorite chords, start them in a low position on your guitar and move them up in minor thirds or start them in a high position and move them down in minor thirds.

Play the exercises below backwards, starting with T1 then 4, 3, 2 and back to the 1 .

LESSON 15

Symetric Introductions and Endings - Part 1

Exercises 36 and 37 are identical to exercises 29C and 30A in their opening bars, but they end with a Symetric Cycle. These Symetric additions give the music a dynamic sound which could never be achieved in Diatonic Harmony.

Practice exercises 36 and 37 and commit them to memory. This done, take the remaining introductions and ending in lesson 12 put the last chord in each example into a Symetric Cycle. If the last chord ends high on the finger board, move it down in minor thirds, if it ends low, move it up.

It is possible to use only fragments of the chord rather than its entirety. As an example go back to lesson 11, exercise 25A. In the second bar the last two beats are diminished, notice this chord glissandos up in minor thirds. In the same bar of exercise 25B it glissandos down in minor thirds. In the 6th bar of both examples it happens again. The same thing occurs in the 3rd bar of exercise 24.

INTRODUCTION

Ex. 36

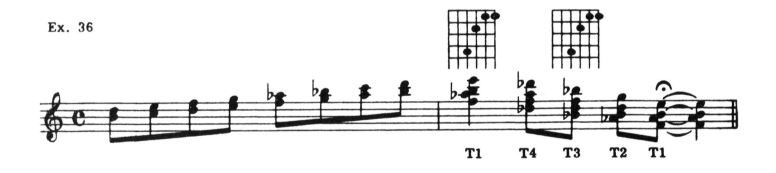

ENDING

Ex. 37

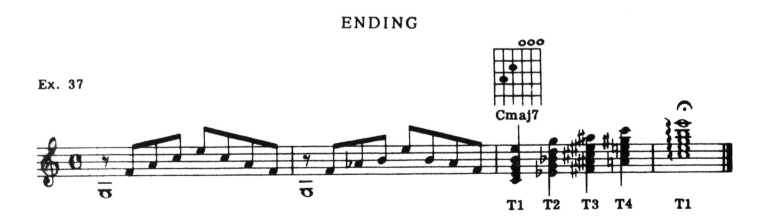

Symetric Introductions and Endings - Part 2

As you shall see in the examples to follow there are many ways to use these Symetric Cycles other than straight up and down in minor thirds.

Practice these variations and commit them to memory. Try using them in introductions and endings in any songs you know.

This is **Ex. 33** in Broken Chords played backwards.

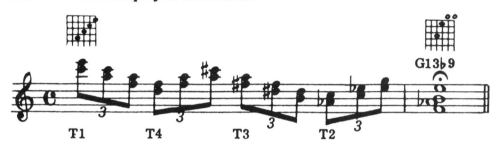

Ex. 34

Ex. 34 Played Backwards

Similar to Ex. 32.

Augmented Cycles

Augmented chords are built on major thirds. A "C" augmented chord has the tones "C", "E" and "G#" (Exercise 38). When this chord is moved up a major third on the finger board, the same tones appear. See Exercise 39.

Divide the 12 tone scale in three equal parts and you get three tonics, T. 1, 2, and 3. Exercise 40 demonstrates the Augmented chord in a Symetric Cycle. It is possible to use the Augmented Cycle in many ways. For instance, exercise 41 is similar to exercise 40, however, now we have six tonics, the additional tonics having been forced into the cycle.

Let me bring out this fact. Symetric Harmony, as we are applying it, moves from one point to another. What goes on between these two points is of no consequence. Harmony is parallel either up or down and you can have as many as 12 tonics (Exercise 42).

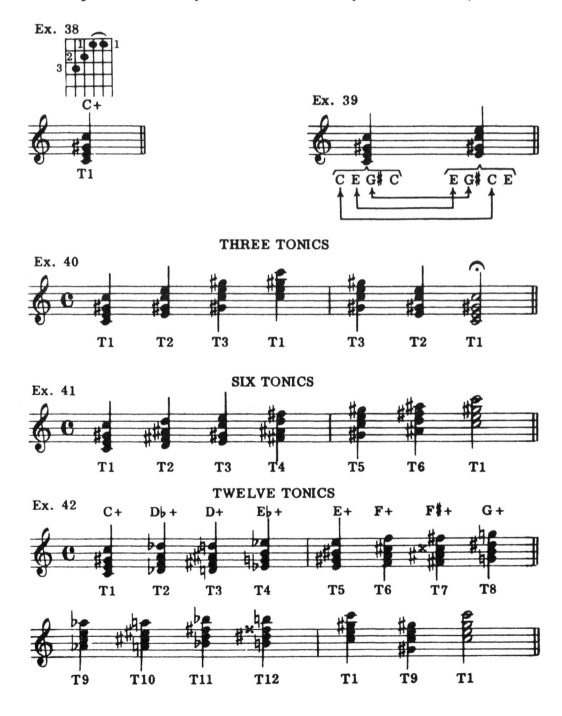

Augmented 7ths

By adding a 7th to the Augmented chord you get still another sound (See Exercise 43). Rather than writing out a lot of cycles, let us analyze a few bars of exercise 26A and B in lesson 11. Exercise 44 shows the Augmented cycles used in the second bars of both A and B in exercise 26. Exercise 45 shows the Augmented cycles used in the 15th and 16th bars of the same exercise. Analyze them thoroughly.

As mentioned in the second paragraph of lesson 11, many chords are used that don't appear in the original chord structure of a song. They are used to add color and originality. See lesson 20 for a more detailed analysis.

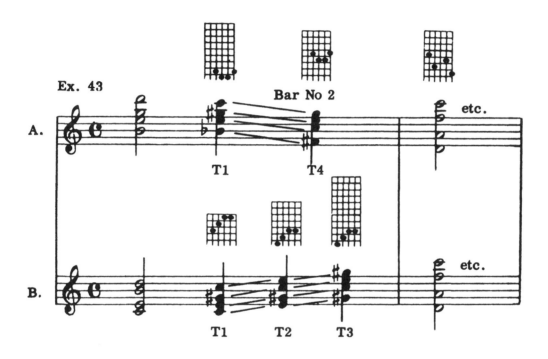

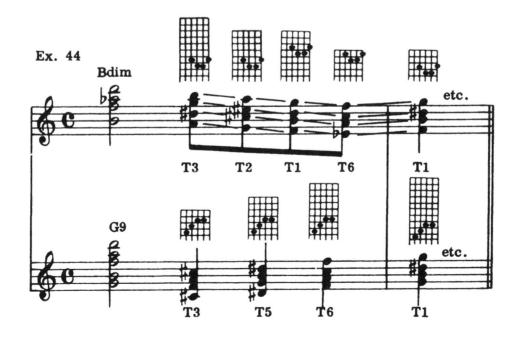

Application of Symetric Cycles
(Rhythmic Chord and Melody Playing)

In this Lesson we have the first eight bars of a number of songs, employing all the chord cycles illustrated up to this point. This is Rhythmic Chord and Melody Playing. It deals with background rather than melody. We will suppose the melody is coming from another source such as a vocalist or an instrument. The guitar plays fill-ins and fragments of melody in the background. This is the best way to use the guitar when working with a small combo such as bass, drums and guitar, or other small combinations. Once you have mastered this type of playing the piano will no longer be a necessity. In fact, today many groups work without the piano.

Practice the following exercises until they are part of you. Be absolute in your study. Memorize every musical thought brought out in each exercise. Bear in mind, that just glancing through this book doesn't mean a thing. It must be studied dilligently over and over again.

WILL YOU STILL BE MINE?

TOM ADAIR
MATT DENNIS

EX. 45

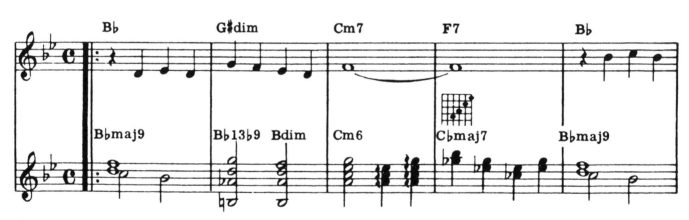

Used by Permission

OH! LOOK AT ME NOW

Ex. 46

JOE BUSHKIN
JOHN DE VRIES

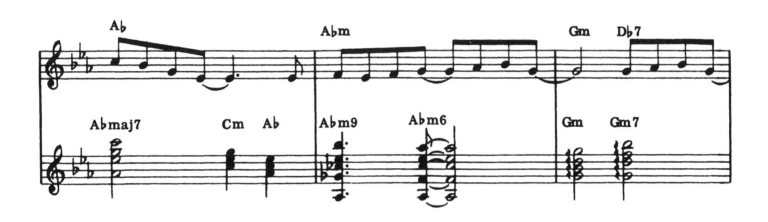

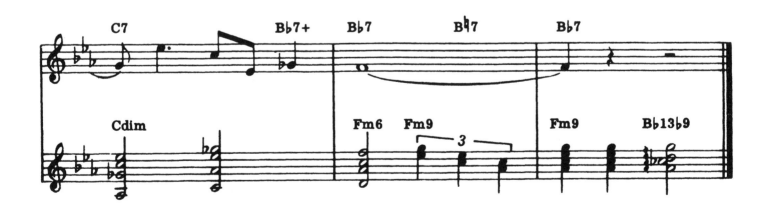

JUST AS THOUGH YOU WERE HERE

Ex. 47

EDGAR DE LANGE
JOHN B. BROOKS

IT STARTED ALL OVER AGAIN

Ex. 48

BILL CAREY
CARL FISHER

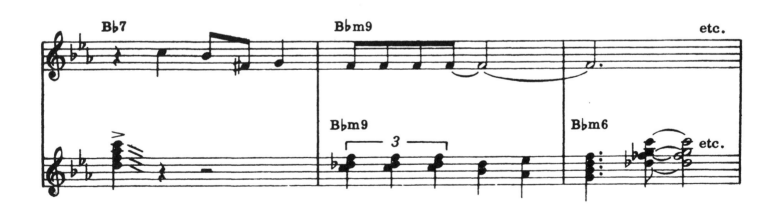

Used by Permission

EVERYTHING HAPPENS TO ME

Ex. 49

TOM ADAIR
MATT DENNIS

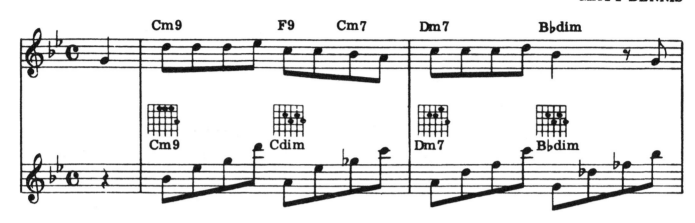

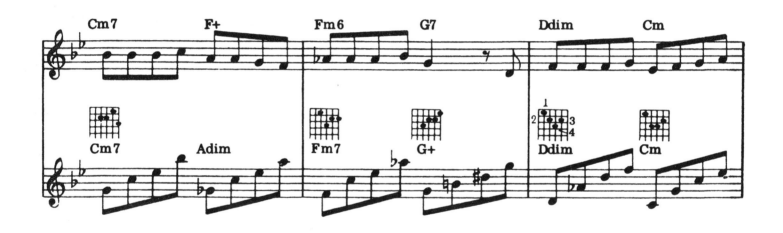

Chord Analysis

Many of the chords that were used in the examples of lesson 19 have multiple names. This fact is evident in many cases of chord and melody playing. The most important of these chords are analyzed in exercise 50. Study the analysis and review lesson 19. Pay minute attention to how chords appear time and time again bearing one name at one point and another the next.

In many cases of chord and melody playing the original chord structure is dropped for certain melodic passages. For example, in exercise 49 all the chords are played arpeggio but the first note of each chord is the most important. It forms a melodic line at the base of the chord and gives the whole example originality. If each of those notes were written out in half tones, you would have a counter melody to the original. See Exercise 65 in Lesson 25.

It is not always possible to harmonize the melody with chords that are familiar to you. At this point it becomes necessary to create chords that will fit the melody and also blend well musically with the chord cycles you are creating. For instance, in the 5th bar of exercise 49, there is a D Diminished chord which is not a standard fingering. However, it does fit well into the pattern used. As you go along you will find it necessary to create chords for effect that may never be useful to you again.

Ex. 50

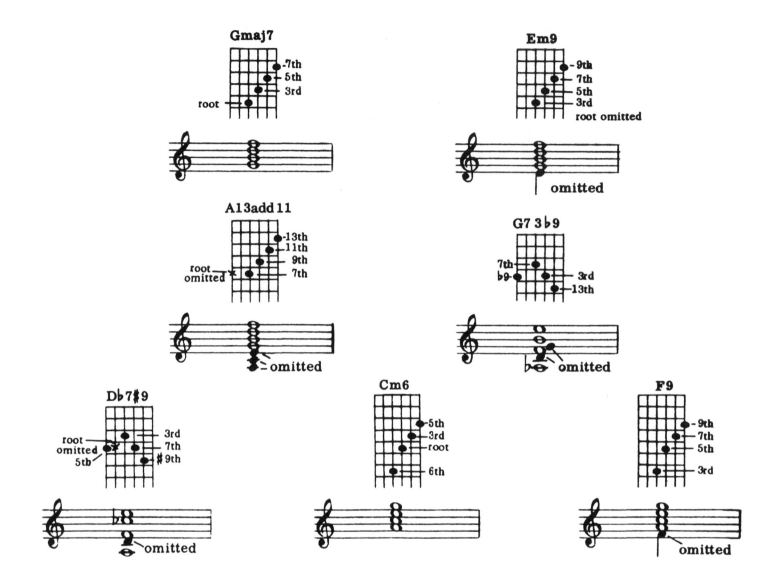

LESSON 21

Diminished & Augmented Resolutions

    Diminished 7th chords resolve beautifully into tonic chords. Actually they aren't diminished chords at all when used in this respect. They are the Upper tones to a diminished or flatted 9th chord. In exercise 51a you have a G7♭9 chord with the root omitted. In 51b you have a B Diminished chord. Analyze the two chords.

    In exercise 52 which is an extraction of exercise 24 in lesson 11, notice how the diminished chord instead of the dominant, resolves into the tonic. Analyze this thoroughly. This is another form of the Altered chord that can be used along with those illustrated in exercise 23 in lesson 10. Augmented chords may be used in a similar manner. See Exercise 53.

These are the 2nd and 3rd bars of Ex. 24 in Lesson No. 11. Here a and b are the equivalent to the V – I Resolution.

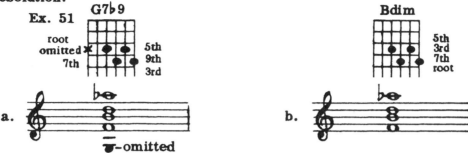

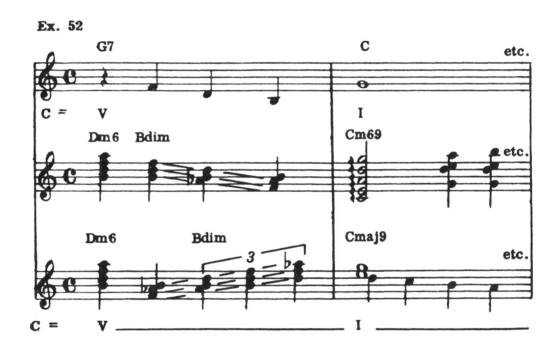

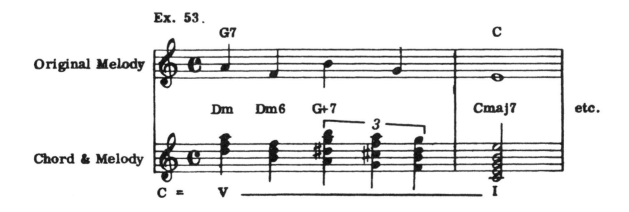

LESSON 22

The Cadence Breaks

As mentioned in Lesson 12, the Cadence Break occurs at the end of a musical thought. Looking through any popular sheet music, you will see that at certain designated points the music relaxes for one or two bars and then either repeats itself or progresses into another musical line. These points are known as the Cadence Breaks (See Exercise 54). Notice that at this Cadence Break the music relaxes on one note for 1 and 3/4 bars. In exercise 55 it relaxes for 1 and 1/4 bars.

Semetric Cycles, Pedal Point and other types of original chord progressions may be employed at these points. The musical thought has ended. Any new chord progressions that may be added give new color and originality. For instance, in exercises 54 and 55 Semetric Cycles are added at the Cadence Breaks.

These are the last three bars of Ex. 25 in Lesson No. 11.

These are the last three bars of Ex. 26 in Lesson No. 11.

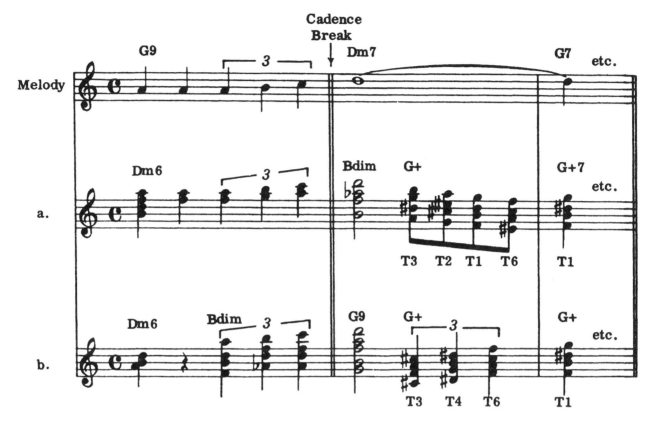

LESSON 23

Pedal Point

A Pedal Point is a sustained or pedal note held or sustained for several measures while a variety of chords are introduced. The most popular note in Pedal Point is the fifth of the scale. In exercise 56 there is an introduction to the key of C Major, the pedal note is G. While the pedal note is being sustained, a Dm9 and a G13♭9 chord play. This is the most popular form of Pedal Point.

To demonstrate Pedal Point on the guitar and to familiarize you with its sound we will use a few tricks. Exercise 57 is an introduction which is to be used in the key of G Major. Lower the 6th string on your guitar a whole tone to D. Practice this exercise until you are thoroughly familiar with the idea and sound of Pedal Point.

There are many ways to play Pedal Point, such as whole notes, half notes, quarter notes and eighth notes. In exercise 58, you lower the 5th string a whole tone to G. This is an introduction to the key of C Major in half note Pedal Point, which fits perfectly to the musical exercise "I Dream of You".

In exercise 59 you raise your 5th string up half a tone to B♭. Here you have an introduction in the key of E♭ using still another variation of Pedal Point.

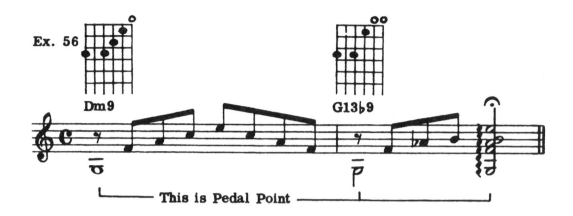

This is Pedal Point

(*) Lower the sixth string to D

Ex. 57

Pedal Point on D, the V of Gmaj.

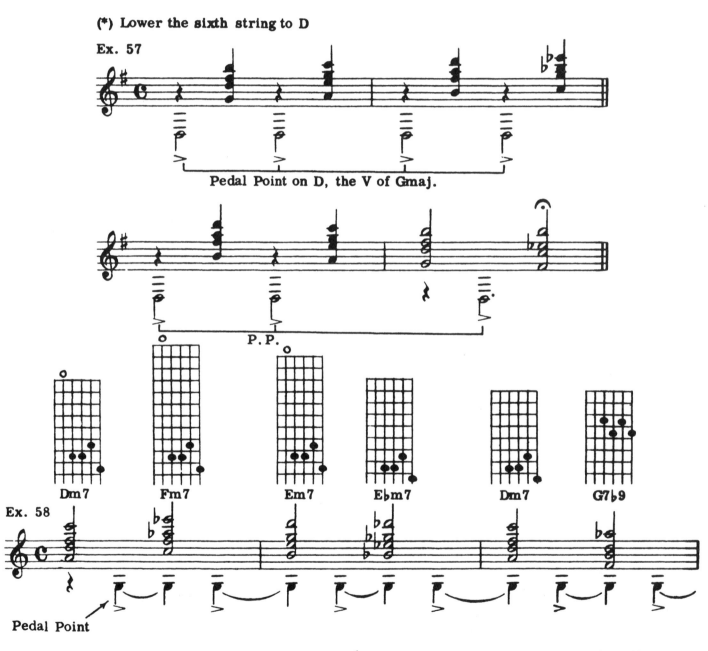

P.P.

Pedal Point

(*) This introduction was taken from Jazz Guitar #1, Ex. 1 in Lesson No. 20. The only difference is that here Pedal Point is added.

Ex. 25 I Dream Of You

A7♭9 Dm6 Dm7 Dm G7 C Cmaj7 etc.

Ex. 59

Pedal Point

Fm9

B♭13 E♭maj7

A7♭9 Fm9

B♭13♭9 Ex. 47 Just As Though You Were Here

E♭ Cm A♭ E7

Practical use of Pedal Point

Exercises 57 and 59 are not practical for playing in public. They were used to demonstrate the sound and feel of Pedal Point.

Pedal Point must be distributed according to the size of the unit or combo with which you are working. In most cases, the bass plays the Pedal Point while the piano or guitar plays the chord variations.

Exercises 60 and 61 illustrate the first few bars of an arrangement with the bass playing Pedal Point, the guitar playing the chord variations and the voice or solo instrument carrying the melody of the song. These are the same introductions used in exercises 58 and 59 of lesson 23.

Pedal Point may also be used at the Cadence Breaks and endings.

Ex. 60

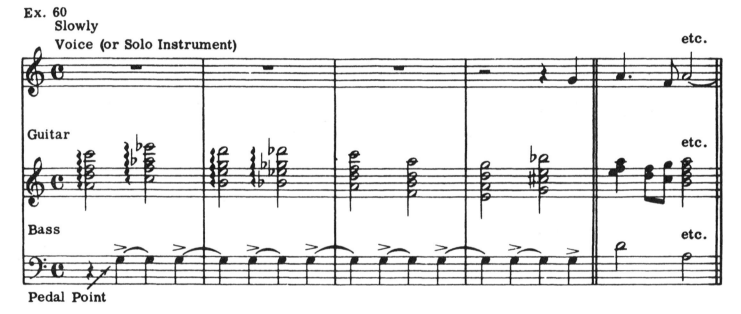

Ex. 61

I'll wake each morn-ing and I'll

LESSON 25

Counterpoint

Counterpoint is, in reality, the movement of two or more melodies rather than the use of chord harmony. It plays a very important part in modern music even though it is from the "Old School". Some small combos derive great benefit from the use of it. In the exercises to follow there are several examples on the application of Counterpoint.

When two lines move against one another that is a form of Counterpoint. There are times when one melody sustains itself for as many as 4 beats, while the other line moves along in quarter or eighth notes. See Exercise 62.

There are many names for these melodies: Cantus Firmus, meaning the original melody; Counterpoint, meaning the added melody, sometimes referred to as the Counter melody. However, these are technical terms and melody and counter melody will suffice. See Exercise 63.

Exercise 64 demonstrates Counterpoint with only two melodies, moving in different directions.

Most of the examples in this book are brief and move chordally from one direction to another. Though they never linger on one note for any length of time, there is never a sign or sound of bad harmonic movement.

Exercise 65 illustrates a melody and counter melody moving along simultaneously. This is the same example in exercise 49 of lesson 19. The difference is that only the first note in each chord of the counter melody is used. This is a sustaining type of counter melody and it offers a strong straight line quality while the melody dances along on top of it.

LESSON 26

SUMMARY

If you analyze all the exercises in this book, past and future, you will note that every passage is well conceived musically. Nothing is left to chance, nothing will misguide you. Many of the exercises are the result of years of study and application.

Symetric Harmony and Counterpoint offer a wealth of ideas to a Jazz musician; I have only opened the door to these subjects. You would do well to study further these musical "Giants".

The exercises to follow put into actual play everything you have studied. Study and analyze them carefully. Pay strict attention to how chords are forced against the melody and, at some points, even dropped for a better melodic line.

With a well rounded musical knowledge and a genuine feeling for Jazz there is no limit to what you can create and play on your guitar.

I THINK OF YOU

Ex. 66

JACK ELLIOT
DON MARCOTTE

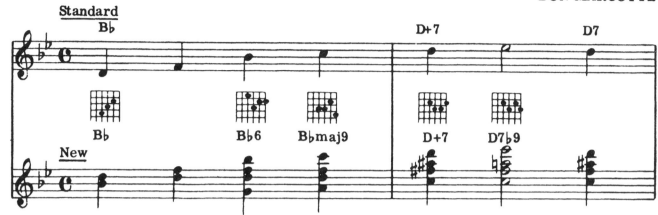

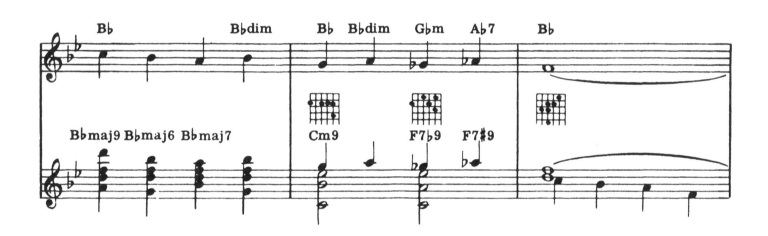

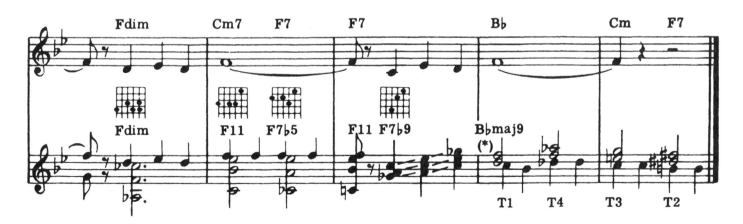

Used by Permission

(*) See Lesson 22, The Cadence Break

I SHOULD CARE

SAMMY CAHN
AXEL STORDAHL
PAUL WESTON

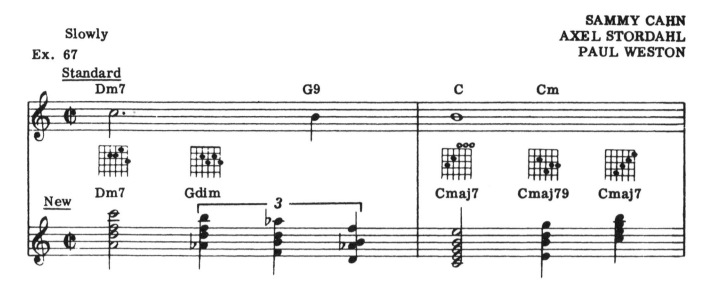

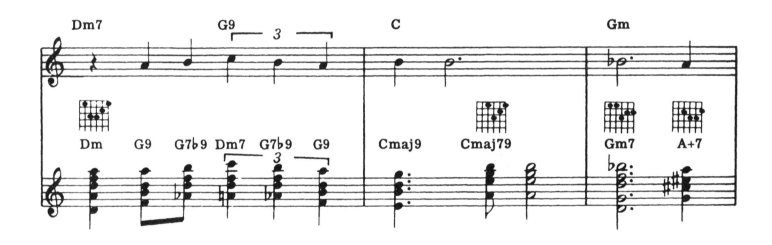

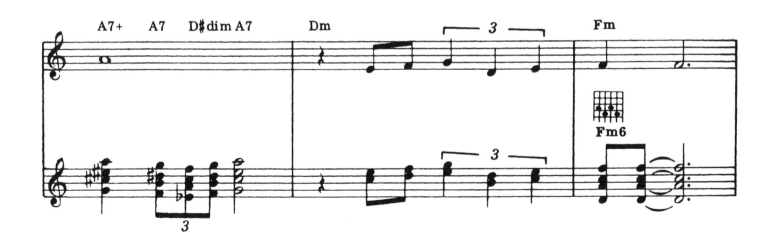

Used by Permission

NEVADA

WALTER DONALDSON
MART GREENE

Ex. 68

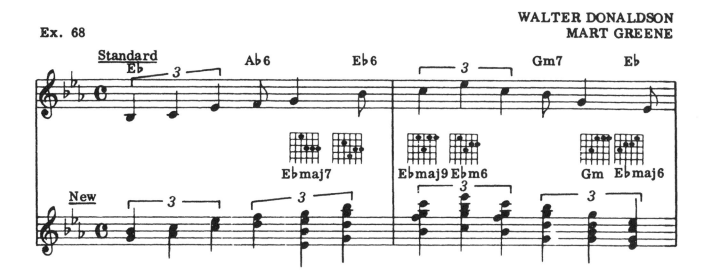

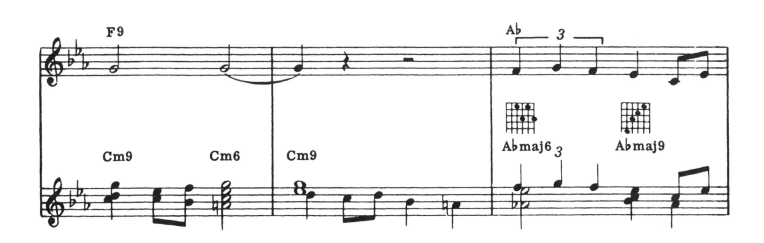

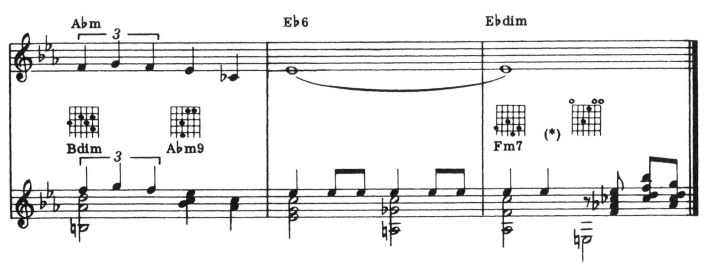

Used by Permission

(*) Symetric cycle

THE NIGHT WE CALLED IT A DAY

TOM ADAIR
MATT DENNIS

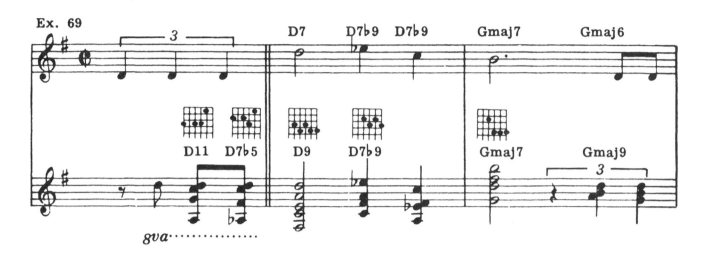

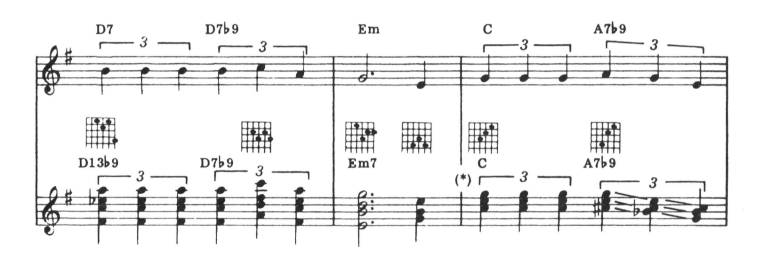

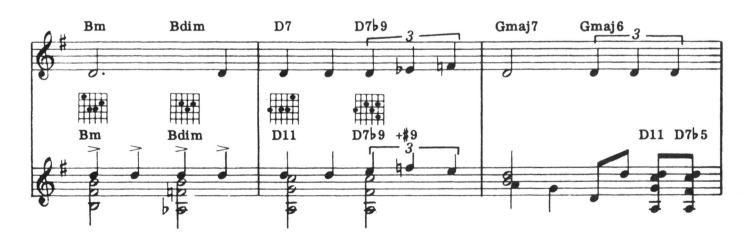

Used by Permission

(*) See Lesson 26, third paragraph.

LOST LAMENT

MICKEY BAKER

(*) See Ex. 56 . Pedal Point

Used by Permission

PATHOS

MICKEY BAKER

Used by Permission

JUST BOBI

MICKEY BAKER

Used by Permission